Soccer Dribbling & Foot Skills:

A Step-by-Step Guide on How to Dribble Past the Other Team

Dylan Joseph

Soccer Dribbling & Foot Skills: A Step-by-Step Guide on How to Dribble Past the Other Team

By: Dylan Joseph

Bonus!

Wouldn't it be nice to have the steps in this book on an easy 1-page printout for you to take to the field? Well, here is your chance!

Go to this Link for an **Instant** 1-Page Printout:
UnderstandSoccer.com/free-printout

This FREE guide is simply a "Thank You" for purchasing this book. This 1-page printout will ensure that the knowledge you obtain from this book makes it to the field.

Table of Contents

About the Author

There I was, a soccer player who had difficulties scoring. I wanted to be the best on the field but lacked the confidence and know-how to make my goal a reality. Every day, I dreamed about improving, but the average coaching and my lack of knowledge only left me feeling alone and like I couldn't attain my goal. I was a quiet player and my performance went unnoticed.

This all changed after my junior year on the Varsity soccer team of one of the largest high schools in the state. During the team and parent banquet at the end of the season, my coach decided to say something nice about each player. When it came to my turn to receive praise, the only thing he came up with was that I had scored two goals that season even though it was against a lousy team, so they didn't really count...

It was a very painful statement that after the 20+ game season, all that could be said of my efforts were two goals that didn't count. Since that moment, I have been forever changed considering one of my greatest fears came true; I was called out in front of my family and friends. Because of that, I got serious. With a new soccer mentor, I focused on the training necessary to obtain the skills to build my confidence and become the goal scorer I always dreamed of being. The next season, after just a few months, I found myself moved up to the starting position of center midfielder and scored my first goal of the 26 game season in only the third game.

I kept up the additional training led by a proven goal scorer to build my knowledge. Fast forward to present day and as a result of the work and focus on the necessary skills, I figured out how to become a goal scorer who averages about two goals and an assist per game, all because of an increase in my understanding of how to play soccer. I was able to take my game from bench-warmer who got called out in front of everybody to the most confident player on the field.

Currently, I am a soccer trainer in Michigan working for Next Level Training. I advanced through their rigorous program as a soccer player and was hired as a trainer. This program has allowed me to guide world-class soccer players for over a decade. I train soccer players in formats ranging from one-hour classes to weeklong camps and from instructing groups of 30 soccer players all the way down to working one-on-one with individuals looking to play for the United States National Team. If you live in the metropolitan Detroit area and want to be the best player in the league, Next Level Training is for you. Learn more at www.next-leveltraining.com. Please leave a review for this book at the end.

Additional Books by the Author that are Available on Amazon:

Soccer Training: A Step-by-Step Guide on 14 Topics for Intelligent Soccer Players, Coaches, and Parents

Soccer Shooting & Finishing: A Step-by-Step Guide on How to Score

Soccer Passing & Receiving: A Step-by-Step Guide on How to Work with Your Teammates

Soccer Defending: A Step-by-Step Guide on How to Stop the Other Team

Dedication

This book is dedicated to all the soccer players, coaches, and parents who are reading this information to increase their confidence, their players' knowledge, and their child's self-esteem. It was not too long ago that I was in the same position as a struggling defensive center midfielder. A "high" scoring season for me was five goals. After obtaining the knowledge and implementing it successfully, it is very realistic for me to score five goals in two games. This statement is not to boast or impress you, but to express that with the correct techniques, you can be or create a goal-scoring machine too.

Also, this book is dedicated to my soccer mentor, Aaron Byrd. Aaron has taught me countless techniques to dribble through the defense. His knowledge has allowed me to create the steps in this book to help you dribble past the other team. I greatly appreciate his awareness of the game, his outstanding work ethic, and his fun personality that makes every single session for the trainees and myself a blast. He is the owner of Next Level Training, a soccer training organization based in the metropolitan Detroit area. If you live in this area and want to be the best player in the league, Next Level Training is for you. Learn more at Next-LevelTraining.com.

Preface

The title of this book is *Soccer Dribbling & Foot Skills*. Average soccer players pass the ball as soon as they receive it, but great soccer players are able to dribble past a defender or two if that is what is needed to help their team score. This book dives deep into how to dribble the ball properly and the different foot skills to use to dribble past the other team. Though the correct form and tactics are helpful in ensuring the ball ends up in the opponent's net, you also need a solid understanding of what skills to use in which situations.

This book gives you the tips, tricks, tweaks, and techniques to become the person on your team that can consistently dribble past players on the other team. Understand that changing one or two things may help improve your game, but once you start implementing most, if not all of the techniques described in this book, you will see a significant improvement in your performance on the field. The knowledge in this book is only helpful when applied. Therefore, apply it to be sure you are dribbling in the appropriate situations by using the most effective and easiest to understand skills to score 10X more goals each season. 10X more goals each season will lead to several more wins every season for your team. For any words that you are unsure of the meaning, please reference the glossary in the back of the book.

INDIVIDUAL SOCCER PLAYER'S PYRAMID

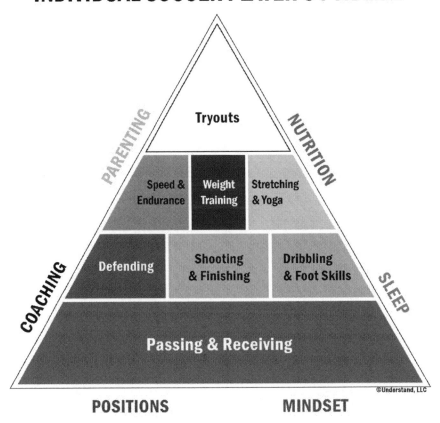

If you are looking to improve your skills, your child's confidence, or your players' abilities, it is essential to understand where this book fits into the bigger picture of developing a soccer player. In the image above, you can see that the most critical field-specific things to work on are at the base of the Individual Soccer Player's Pyramid. Note: A team's pyramid may look slightly different based on the tactics the players can handle and the approach the coach decides to use for games. The pyramid is a quality outline when you are looking to improve an individual soccer player's game. All of the elements in the pyramid and the items surrounding it play a meaningful part in becoming a better player, but certain things should be read and mastered first before moving on to other topics.

You will notice that passing & receiving is at the foundation of the pyramid because if you can receive a pass and make a pass in soccer, you will be a useful teammate. Though you may not be the one that is consistently scoring, the person that is dispossessing the other team, or the player that can dribble through several opponents, you will have the fundamental tools needed to play the sport and contribute to your team.

As you move one layer up, you find yourself with a decision to make on how to progress. Specifically, the pyramid is created with you in mind because each soccer player and each soccer position has different needs. Therefore, your choice regarding which path to take first is dictated by the position you play and more importantly, by the position that you want to play. In soccer and life, just because you are in a particular spot, position, or even a job, it does not mean that you have to stay there forever if that is not your choice. However, it is not recommended to refuse playing a position if you are not in the exact role you want. It takes time to develop the skills that will allow you to make a shift from one position to another.

If you are a forward or if you want to become one, then consider your route on the second layer of the pyramid to start with shooting & finishing. As your abilities to shoot increase, your coach will notice your new finishing skills and be more likely to move you up the field if you are not a forward already. Be sure to communicate to the coach that you desire to be moved up the field to a more offensive position, which will increase your chances as well. If you are already a forward, then dive deep into this topic to ensure you become the leading scorer on your team and in the entire league. Notice that shooting & finishing is considered less critical than passing & receiving because you have to pass the ball up the field before you can take a shot on net.

Otherwise, you can start by progressing to dribbling & foot skills from passing & receiving because the proper technique is crucial to dribble the ball well. It is often necessary for a soccer player to use a skill to protect the ball from the other team or to advance the ball up the field to place their team in a favorable situation to score. The selection of this route is often taken first by midfielders and occasionally by forwards.

Defending is another option of how you can proceed from passing & receiving. Being able to keep the other team off the scoreboard is not an easy task. Developing a defender's mindset, learning which way to push a forward, understanding how to position your body, knowing when to foul, and using the correct form for headers is critical to a defender on the back line looking to prevent goals.

Finish all three areas in the second layer of the pyramid before progressing up the pyramid. Dribbling and defending the ball (not just shooting) are useful for an attacker, shooting and defending (not just dribbling) are helpful for a midfielder, while shooting and dribbling (not just defending) are helpful for a defender. Having a well-rounded knowledge of the skills needed for the different positions is important for all soccer players. It is especially essential for those soccer players looking to change positions in the future. Shooting & finishing, dribbling & foot skills, and defending are oftentimes more beneficial for soccer players to learn first than the next tier of the pyramid, so focus on these before spending time on areas higher up in the pyramid. In addition, reading about each of these areas will help you to understand what your opponent wants to do as well.

Once you have improved your skills at the 1st and 2nd tiers of the pyramid, move upwards to fitness. As you practice everything below this category on the pyramid, your fitness and strength will naturally increase. It is difficult to go through a passing/dribbling/finishing drill for a few minutes without being out of breath. Performing the technical drills allows soccer players to increase their fitness naturally. This reduces the need to focus exclusively on running for fitness. Coming from a soccer player and trainer (someone with a view from both sides), I know that a constant focus on running is not as fulfilling and does not create long-lasting improvements. Whereas, emphasizing the shooting capabilities, foot skills, and defending knowledge of a soccer player does create long-lasting change. Often, the coaches that focus on running their players in practice are the coaches that care to improve their team but have limited knowledge of many of the soccer-specific topics that would quickly increase their players' abilities. Not only does fitness in soccer include your endurance, but it also addresses your ability to run with agility and speed, develop strength and power, while improving your flexibility through stretching and yoga to become a well-rounded soccer player.

Similarly to the tier below it, you should focus on the fitness areas that will help you specifically, while keeping all of the topics in mind. For example, you may be a smaller soccer player that could use some size. Then, you would emphasize weight training and gain the muscle to avoid being pushed off the ball. However, you would still want to stretch before and after a lifting workout or soccer practice/game to ensure that you stay limber and flexible, so that you can recover quickly and avoid injuries.

Maybe you are a soccer player in your 20s, 30s, or 40s. Then, emphasizing your flexibility and practicing a bit of yoga would do a world of good to ensure you keep playing soccer for many more years. However, doing a few sets of push-ups, pull-ups, squats, lunges, sit-ups, etc. per week will help you maintain or gain a desirable physique.

Furthermore, you could be in the prime of your career in high school, college, or at a pro level, which would mean that obtaining the speed and endurance to run for 90+ minutes is the most essential key to continue pursuing your soccer aspirations.

Finally, we travel to the top of the pyramid which involves tryouts. Though tryouts occur only one to two times per year, they have a huge impact on whether you make the team you want to join or get left out of the lineup. Tryouts can cause intense nerves if you do not know the keys to making sure that you stand out and a very confident from the start.

If you have not read *Soccer Training: A Step-by-Step Guide*, it is highly recommended that you do to gain general knowledge of the crucial topics within the areas of the pyramid. Furthermore, there are a few soccer terms that are described in detail in the *Soccer Training* book that may only be referenced in this book. Picking up a copy of the book will act as a good gauge to see how much you know about each topic. This will help to determine if a book later in the series written about a specific subject in the soccer pyramid will be beneficial for you.

The last portion of the pyramid are the areas that surround the pyramid. Though these are not skills and topics that can be addressed by your physical abilities, they each play key roles in rounding out a complete soccer player. For example, having a supportive parent/guardian or two is beneficial for transporting the child to games, providing the equipment needed, the fees for the team, expenses for individual training, and encouragement. Having a quality coach will help the individual learn how their performance and skills fit into the team's big picture.

Sleeping enough is critical to having energy in practices and on game days, in addition to recovering from training and games. Appropriate soccer nutrition will increase the energy and endurance of a soccer player, help the soccer player achieve the ideal physique, and significantly aid in the recovery of the athlete. Understanding soccer positions will help to determine if a specific role is well-suited given your skills. It is important to know that there are additional types of specific positions, not just forwards, midfielders, and defenders. A former or current professional player in the same position as yours can provide you guidance on the requirements of effectively playing that position. Last, but not least, is developing a mindset that leaves you unshakable. This mindset will help you become prepared for game situations, learn how to deal with other players, and be mentally tough enough to not worry about circumstances that you cannot control, such as the type of field you play on, the officiating, or the weather. The pyramid is a great visual aid to consider when choosing what areas to read next as a soccer player, coach, or parent. Now that you know where this book plays into the bigger picture, let us begin.

If you enjoy this book, please leave a review on Amazon letting me know.

Chapter 1

How to Dribble Effectively

In soccer, being a confident dribbler is key to advancing your abilities as a soccer player. If you work towards and become a soccer player that can consistently move the ball up the field with your foot skills, you will be a very productive member of any team. To dribble correctly, ensure that you are dribbling with speed. **To dribble with speed, have your toes down and in, pushing off the ground using the balls of your foot (i.e., the portion of the bottom of your foot just below the toes).** If someone ever asks you to stand on your tippy toes, he or she is really asking you to stand on your toes and balls of your feet.

The reason a soccer player does not want to be flat-footed when dribbling is for the same reason a soccer player does not want to run flat-footed. The soccer player will go too slowly and effective dribblers use their agility provided from being on their toes to beat defenders. If you ever watch the fastest soccer players or even the sprinters in the Olympics, you will notice that they run on the balls of their feet to fully engage their calf muscles to be as quick as possible.

Sadly, running on the balls of my feet was not something I figured out until college. In fact, to practice running properly, I would run from class to class focusing exclusively on running with proper form to make sure I could transition to being a faster runner on the field. The other people at the university thought I was a bit odd, given that I was the only person that anyone ever saw running outside of a gym or field, but I was determined to become a faster and more explosive runner. Being able to meet two objectives at once makes it a lot easier to improve and grow more rapidly. In this example, I had to go to class (objective one) and I wanted to improve my speed and running form (objective two).

Getting back to the dribbling form, having the positioning of your foot with your toes down and in, while curling just your toes up (not your ankle) will allow you to essentially **create a "scooper" with your foot** to ensure that you have an accurate push of the ball every time you make contact with it. This form is ideal because it allows you to use the same running form as if you did not have the ball while maintaining the correct contact with the ball using the bone of the top of your foot. Proper form when dribbling guarantees precision with every touch and enough power to dribble the ball with speed.

Pushing the ball with the inside of your foot forces you to point your foot outwards. An outward pointed foot slows down your speed drastically when running, which makes dribbling with the inside of your foot unreasonable. Dribbling with the outside of your foot points your toes too far inward, which makes it equally as unreasonable to dribble with the outside of the foot. **Dribbling with your toes down and slightly pointed in is the**

happy medium to allow you to dribble quickly while running.

Also, when you go to push the ball when the defender is very close to you, do not just push it straight on the ground past the defender. Instead, flick the ball up in the air a little bit. Flicking the ball will give you an increased probability of dribbling by the defender because the ball is more likely to travel past the defender by going over their foot. **Use a slight flick in your push after doing a skill, like a jab step or a scissor, to move the ball over any outstretched legs.** If you flick it, so the ball slightly bounces, you can continue to dribble without any wasted time. Furthermore, flicking the ball past the defender's foot, so that it jumps a bit, will allow you to hit a rocket of a shot. You can strike a powerful shot with a bouncing ball because you can make complete contact with the ball while the ball is bouncing and there is no friction between the ball and the ground that also slows a shot.

Chapter 2

Dribbling with Speed vs. Speed Dribbling

Dribbling for many players consists of taking a touch of the ball every step. A touch every step does not often lead to dribbling with speed and is not efficient in many situations. **Dribbling with speed involves taking a touch only when necessary, but relying heavily on bigger touches and your speed to travel faster in less time.** Understanding this is so critical because you are faster without the ball than you are with the ball. Therefore, the more touches you take with the ball, the slower you will be.

An example I often use with my trainees is that I will tell them that I am going to travel 10 yards in two different ways. The first way I proceed to show them is to take five touches while dribbling the 10 yards. The trainees are then able to observe the time it takes for this option. Next, I travel the 10 yards with one touch. They see that it is two to three times quicker because less touches take less time. Take Gareth Bale who has played for Tottenham, Real Madrid, and the Wales National Team. He understands that his strength is his speed, so he is unafraid to push the ball far out in front of him, which allows his legs to really run.

Therefore, when traveling with the ball in a game or practice, it is essential to take bigger touches that allow you to run after the ball when you are attacking. **When you have space on the field, travel through the area as quickly as possible with only one or two touches. Therefore, dribbling with speed means that you are judging the situation and taking an appropriate amount of touches based on the space you have available.**

Dribbling with speed effectively allows you to bait players on the other team. When you push the ball out in front of you as you are attacking forward, larger pushes bait defenders in. Specifically, pushing the ball several yards away gives defenders the hope that they will be able to intercept the ball or slide tackle it away. A professional that does this very well is Cristiano Ronaldo. He effectively uses his speed and large dribbles in order to bait defenders into over-committing themselves for the ball, which allows him to have a last-second push of the ball away from the opposition.

As previously mentioned, dribbling with speed is pushing the ball many steps forward before taking another touch whereas **speed dribbling is taking a touch every step, but every step is a full running stride to ensure you are traveling as fast as possible with the ball**. An example of a professional that does this exceptionally well is Lionel Messi. Messi is outstanding at being able to run basically as fast while speed dribbling as he is taking one large touch into space and sprinting after the ball. His ability to dribble others is out of this world and he is very efficient in the skills he uses, something that will be talked more about later in this book.

Speed dribbling is something to be practiced so that it can be perfected. It is essential to find the balance between the control needed to run with a ball, but being able to run at the same speed without the ball. Speed dribbling gives you the ability to take a touch with every step, which is vital to be able to adjust your run with the ball as the defenders reveal what they are doing to take the ball from you. **If a defender lunges or slides for the ball, you are more easily able to do a skill to** avoid the oncoming defender than you would be able to with dribbles that travel a significant distance in one push.

Soccer players looking to advance their game will work to become great at **dribbling with speed (taking a large touch to cover several yards with one touch) and speed dribbling (being able to sprint while pushing the ball with every step of the foot that is dribbling the ball)**. Most players learn speed dribbling, but do not learn about dribbling with speed. Combine these both and raise your abilities past those of your opponents and even your teammates.

Chapter 3

How to React Based on a Defender's Stance

When attacking a defender, do you ever wonder how you should read their body language to make it easier for you to dribble past them? **Well, based on their positioning in front of you, in addition to their stance (which way their hips are facing), you can determine what direction they are looking to force you to travel.** Additionally, it can reveal if they lack the correct defending technique. A good defender will force you in the direction they want you to go. A great attacker will go in the direction that gives him or her the highest probability of success. A great attacker will likely be able to go both ways, but he or she will want to assess the situation and determine which direction will make it easier for him or her to strike a shot or complete a pass.

In the first book of this Understand Soccer Series, *Soccer Training: A Step-by-Step Guide on 14 Topics for Intelligent Soccer Players, Coaches, and Parents*, we discussed what an appropriate stance for a defender is. A defender that wants you to go to your right should have their right foot slightly in front of their left foot so that their hips are pointing diagonally to the left. The defender should not be directly in front of the attacker but slightly off to the attackers left side creating more space for the attacker to dribble up the field to the right. The reverse applies when a defender wants to give you space to your left. Keep in mind that not all defenders position themselves properly. **If a defender is directly in front of you and has their hips turned to the right, attack to the left.** If they have their hips turned to the left, then attack to the right because it will take more time and it will be slower for them to transition from their hips pointing one way to turn and sprint in the other direction.

Now that you understand correct positioning for a defender let us consider options when attacking. **If a defender gives you space to your opposite foot, take it.** This is granted you are comfortable shooting or passing with your opposite foot. If the defender is directly in front of you and turned to the right or the left, attack the opposite direction they are facing, all other things being equal. If the defender's hips are pointed directly at you and not turned to the right or left at all, then attack in the direction that will give you an easier shot on net or a pass to a teammate. If they have square hips this is one of the easiest times for you to do a nutmeg. However, see the chapter on nutmegs to find out why it is still not the best idea to pursue. If the defender has an additional supporting defender, they would want to be pushing you into that supporting defender.

To conclude, as a dribbler looking to take advantage of a defender's stance, attack the direction the defender is not facing if they are positioned directly in front of you. If the defender is slightly off to one side and not straight in front of you, then attack in the direction they are giving you more space to dribble in. **However, if they are forcing you to your opposite foot and you are not yet experienced enough to use it, then consider trying to attack to your dominant foot, knowing that you are making it more difficult for yourself, given that you cannot use both feet.** Some moves to accomplish this are the jab step, scissor, or shot fake using the inside of the foot to help create space to enable you to travel to your dominant foot, which are all discussed in great detail in later chapters of this book. An excellent example of this was the UEFA Champions League match of Barcelona versus Bayern Munich, where Lionel Messi effectively attacked Jerome Boateng's stance. The result was a goal for Barcelona and a very memorable Boateng tripping over himself in the process.

Chapter 4

Tier 1 – Jab Steps, Self-Passes, & Shot Fakes

Bruce Lee, the famous martial artist and philosopher, once said: "I fear not the man who has practiced 10,000 kicks once, but I fear the man who has practiced one kick 10,000 times." What he is saying is do not settle with being okay by dabbling with many skills in many different areas. He recommends you to be the best in only one thing. **When it comes to soccer, it means pick one skill for each of the different circumstances in a game that you would encounter while dribbling the soccer ball and develop those skills and ONLY those.**

Therefore, the BIG 3 skills that are recommended for all soccer players to develop are the jab step, self-pass, and shot fake. If you subscribed to the UnderstandSoccer.com email list, then this chapter will look familiar. If not, it is highly recommended to subscribe to it for tips, tricks, tweaks, and techniques emailed to you about one time per week. Also, you will have updates on the next book in the series and I have been known to give away books for free.

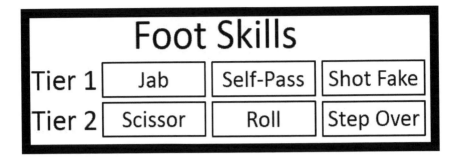

First, the jab step goes by many names: the shoulder drop, the fake, the fake and take, the feint, the body feint, or whatever else you would like to call it. The name is not essential, but mastering the skill is crucial. This skill is by far the best attacking move to use when a defender is backpedaling and you are looking to dribble by him or her. Now, keep in mind that any skill is just to make the defender off balance for a split second. A split second where the defender thinks that you are going in one direction when you intend to take the ball in another direction. However, it is the explosive change of speed after the skill that buys you more time than performing the jab step with the appropriate form. **A good jab step involves the ball starting outside your shoulder and turning your toe down and in to make it look like you will push/dribble the ball.**

Some soccer players may prefer to use the scissor or the step over in this game situation. **Yet, the jab step allows you to make no contact whatsoever with the ball and does not require any extra body positioning that involves additional**

steps similar to that of a scissor. Additionally, this is not the correct time at all to be doing a step over. A correctly performed scissor requires that you step your plant foot past the ball so that you can turn at the hips, which will allow the ball to roll through your legs while the defender is off balance, allowing you to push the ball and attack in the opposite direction that you had faked going. The extra step in a scissor to correctly have your body positioned past the ball takes extra time versus a jab step.

Let us use a very well-known player to demonstrate this further - Lionel Messi. Some would argue that he is or is not the best soccer player, however, there is not much of an argument when someone says he is the best dribbler in the world. **When you watch him, it does not look like he is doing a bunch of skills to dribble past the defenders since it looks so effortless. However, upon further inspection, you will see that he is using the most efficient skills, which he has perfected.** He uses the most efficient skills to score more goals, tally more assists, and increase the chance that his team wins.

Again, this is not to say that the other skills are bad, it is just that they are not as likely to work. Think about it this way, if you do a jab step and you have a 90% success rate, whereas when you perform a scissor, you have an 80% success rate. **The jab step is a better option because you will have a higher percentage of successes with that skill because it takes less time than the scissor.** An example of the quality of the jab step is that during one of the previous Next Level Training soccer summer camps that I was a trainer at, there was a girl that followed my advice in a drill that we were doing. The drill was simply 1v1s and you had to travel to the other side of the grid for a point. The player, Emily, did the same jab step nine times in a row and it worked every single time.

Next, the self-pass is a very effective skill when the defender is reaching in for the ball. Anytime he or she is reaching towards you to take the ball away, it naturally means their momentum is going towards you and your momentum is going in the opposite direction. This means you do not need to fake the ball one way and take it another way when the opposing player is lunging toward the ball. Simply move the ball out of the way. The self-pass is also known as an "L", an Iniesta, or a la croqueta. It is as easy as passing the ball from one foot to the other, straight across the defender's body. Notice that it said "across the defender's body" and not across your own body. Going "across the defender's body" is critical because we do not want the ball traveling diagonally in relation to the defender because then it moves the ball closer to them, which makes it easier for them to steal the ball than if we moved the ball straight across him or her. Remember, the first portion of the self-pass is the bottom of an "L," which will make it a lot easier to dribble the ball by the defender.

Lastly, you can perform a shot fake in various ways. You can perform your shot fake using a Cruyff, a step on step out, a jump turn, a V pull back, an outside of the foot cut, or an inside of the foot cut. Each of which has an appropriate time to use in a game. **Being very convincing with a shot fake allows you to buy that half second of time where the defender flinches (if they are a few yards from you) or where the defender dives in (if they are closer to you).** Either one allows you to dribble in the other direction, pass, or find room to shoot. Furthermore, your shot fake must look exactly like what? Your shot! Ensure that your arms, leg, and head all go up the same way when performing a shot fake or a shot.

Develop these BIG 3 skills to take your game to the next level. Say that you prefer the scissor over the jab step. That is fine, but make sure to practice it nonstop to ensure you are the best at the scissor. Do not waste time and effort trying to learn all the fancy skills that show up on SportsCenter highlights and in the Top 10 Plays. **In reality, practicing the complex moves decreases the amount of time spent on moves you know you can use successfully every game.** The "fancy" skills do not produce the same amount of results that the other, fundamental but very efficient skills do. Right now is an important time in your soccer career, so decide if you want to be a fancy player or if you want to be a player that scores a lot of goals. For the most part, they are not the same player.

Obviously, if you begin to excel with your BIG 3 skills and you are now able to dribble several defenders at once, like Lionel Messi, it will look fancy. **Therefore, now is the time to decide if you want to be the player that scores two goals a game and may have a few, if any, fancy goals over the course of a season or would you rather be that player that scores a few very spectacular goals a season because you want to use too much practice time on skills that are not efficient?** Choose wisely and choose now as you want to take the time to perfect the skills that you will use for years to come.

Chapter 5

Tier 2 – Scissor, Rolls, & Step Overs

We just discussed the Tier 1 skills that can be performed in the previous chapter. **Use the jab step when a defender is backpedaling, a self-pass when the defender is overcommitting and reaching in for the ball, and the shot fake when you are hoping to have the defender either flinch or lunge in the wrong direction.** Now let us take a look at the Tier 2 skills. The skills in this chapter are considered Tier 2 skills because they are not quite as important or useful as the Tier 1 skills, but can be a useful part of a soccer player's skill set.

The three moves that are considered Tier 2 soccer skills are the scissor, the roll, and the step over. For many players, when they are initially learning to do the scissor, they end up moving their leg and their foot over the ball. The motion they make is similar to that of a magician moving his wand over his hat during the magic trick of pulling a rabbit out of his hat. The "magic wand" motion is not good form and is not believable at all. Many people that teach a scissor tell the soccer player to reach their leg out for the ball, to go around the ball with their leg in a circular motion, and then push the ball away with the opposite foot. **The problem with this is if you are reaching forward for the ball to go around it with your foot, your hips**

never change direction, so the defender is not going to be faked out.

A good defender is going to be watching the ball just as much as they are watching your hips and if you are not showing that you plan to go one way with your body, they will not believe your scissor. Therefore, the trick when doing the scissor is to have your plant foot planted past the ball so that you just have to take a step past the ball with your other leg as it is rolling through your legs while you are dribbling the ball. **In a sense, a scissor is really just a jab step in front of the ball.** The reason that the scissor is a Tier 2 skill and the jab step is a Tier 1 skill is that even though they are used in the same situation when a defender is backpedaling, the scissor takes an extra step in order to step past the ball and that extra step takes extra time. As a result, a scissor is not as quick as a jab step and if you were only to practice one of these skills, it is highly recommended that it be the jab step.

There is a difference between a scissor and a double scissor. A scissor is when you only use one leg whereas a double scissor is when you use one leg to go around the ball and then you use the opposite leg as well to go around the ball, hence the "double" in a double scissor. **When doing a scissor, if you do a right-footed scissor, you are faking to the right, so you should be pushing the ball away with your left foot and pushing it towards the left.** If you push it towards the right, you are faking in the direction that you are ultimately going, so you are telling the defender where you will go and then you will likely push it right into their shins.

Also, the reason that you should use the opposite foot to push the ball away is that it takes one less step. Using fewer steps will take less time and make you a quicker soccer player. If you perform a scissor with one foot and push it away with that same foot, it requires you to take three steps. The first step is the scissor, the second step with the opposite leg is to plant, and then the third step is to push the ball away with the same leg that did the scissor. Why add an extra step if it will only take extra time? If you do a right-footed scissor and you are faking to go to the right, then push it away with your left, which only takes two steps and then proceed to accelerate after your push.

The next Tier 2 move is the roll. The roll is to be performed with the bottom of your toes, but the problem with the roll is that you have to take your foot from the ground to the top of the ball, roll the ball, which crosses your feet, then uncross your feet, and take a touch forward with your opposite foot. Similarly to the self-pass, a roll is used when a defender is reaching in for the ball and you are just simply pushing the ball out of the way of their foot and then accelerating past the defender. **Because you are crossing your legs and taking the time to move your foot from the ground to the top of the**

ball, the roll is less athletic and more time-consuming than the self-pass, which is why it is a Tier 2 move. However, the roll does provide a bit more control of the ball than the self-pass provides. Now, keep in mind that any time you do a roll or a self-pass, the ball should be going across the defender and then past them so the path the ball takes is the shape of an "L." Too often players will roll the ball diagonally, which only moves the ball closer to the defender's foot and makes it much easier for the defender to poke the ball away or to fully dispossess you.

The last skill of Tier 2 is the step over. **The step over is best used when your back is facing the direction that you need to go. Never use it when you are attacking forward at a defender that is backpedaling.** Many soccer players mistakenly call a scissor a step over, but they are different. With a scissor, the foot closest to the ball would be the one that goes around the ball. With the step over, as you are standing next to the ball, the leg farthest from the ball steps over the ball. Then, you bring your other leg around in order to plant your legs on the opposite side of the ball to push the ball away with the leg that initially started the step over. To perform the step over correctly, fully turn your shoulders in the direction you want the defender to believe that you are going in order to fake them in the wrong direction.

A step over is an excellent way to fake out a defender when they are on your back. **The step over makes them believe that you are going in one direction, but you intentionally miss the ball completely, so that you can push it out and accelerate with speed in the other direction.** The reason that this is also considered a Tier 2 move is because there are a lot fewer situations in a game that this skill will be needed when compared to the Tier 1 moves of a jab step, a self-pass, or a shot fake. However, this is a great move to have in your skill-set and is not similar to the other skills that we have discussed so far. Therefore, this move is one to practice.

In conclusion, a self-pass is going to be quicker than a roll, which is why a roll is a Tier 2 skill. Similarly, a scissor is going to be slower than a jab step. There are not as many opportunities in a game to use a step over, but it is still effective to do, so that you can dribble out of high-pressure situations with your back facing the direction of the field that you need to go in order to score.

Chapter 6

Tier 1 - Cuts & Shot Fakes

Now, we will be discussing the different types of shot fakes and cuts that you can use as a soccer player. First, a cut is a shot fake without actually faking the shot. **A cut is used to stop the ball from going one direction so you can quickly push the ball in another direction.** By pretending to kick the ball with any of the cuts that we are about to discuss, you will then turn that cut into a shot fake.

With a shot fake, it is critical to remember that a shot fake must look exactly like a shot. This means your arms must go up and your shooting leg must go up exactly the same way as a real shot when you perform a shot fake. If the form is not exactly the same, it might work the first and maybe even the second time, but after that, the defender will recognize the differences in your form and will not be faked out by your shot fakes anymore. Frequently, trainees' shot fakes are not believable because they are not raising their arms as big and they are not bringing their back leg as far back as if they were actually to shoot the ball. Therefore, make your shot and your shot fake look exactly the same so that you will more easily dribble past your opponent.

Shot Fakes		
Tier 1	Step On Step Out	Cut	Chop
Tier 2	Cruyff	V Pull Back	Jump Turn

The first shot fake that I often teach my trainees is the step on step out shot fake. A step on step out shot fake is simply pretending to shoot the ball, then stepping on it with the bottom of your foot instead of striking the ball. Then, with the same foot that stepped on the ball, take another step to plant to the side of the ball, so that your other leg can come through and push the ball in a different direction. **This step on step out is a great attacking shot fake because the entire time, your body and hips are still pointed in the direction you are looking to go up the field.** Whereas with many of the other shot fakes, you end up changing directions completely, so that if you were going forward and you performed a Cruyff on the ball, you would end up turning around and go in a backward direction. As we discussed in the previous chapter, when you stop the ball with the bottom of your foot, use the bottom of your toes to reach farther for the ball and to have the best feel for the ball once you make contact with it.

Another shot fake that is very useful is just cutting the ball with the inside of your foot. As the ball is moving on the field, pretend to shoot it but instead of striking it, just cut it with the inside of your foot so that it either stops, allowing you to push it quickly and accelerate away or cut it, so it starts to move in the opposite direction, so that you can also continue to accelerate away at speed. **A cut shot fake involves the ball staying in front of you, which is different from the Cruyff,** that we will be discussing in the next chapter. Because the ball is staying in front of you, this shot fake is better used when you have 2-3 yards between you and the defender.

If the defender is very close to you, then cutting the ball with the inside of your foot is not the best choice. The Cruyff is better to use because it will allow you to have the ball behind your body, which means you are between the defender and the ball to allow you to protect the ball more easily. With all shot fakes including a cut shot fake, it is beneficial to stop the ball because you know exactly where the ball will be and it makes it easier for you to push the ball away and accelerate after performing the cut shot fake. The disadvantage with the cut shot fake is that if the defender is too close to you, the defender will likely be able to reach the ball and take possession from you.

Therefore, the advantage of cutting the ball where it continues to move after changing direction is that you can cut it away from the defender's reach. However, the disadvantage of cutting the ball with it traveling in the direction you are about to go is that the ball will be further away from you. If you misjudge the defender's movement or do not see another defender on the opposing team, you will be less likely to protect the ball because it is now further away from your body.

Next, doing a shot fake where you cut the ball with the outside of your foot instead of the inside may also be referred to as a chop shot fake. **Performing a chop shot fake is excellent if you are looking to explode in the complete opposite direction you are currently going.** When performing a chop shot fake, it is vital that when you reach for the ball, you have the outside of your foot entirely past the ball and planted on the ground, so that the ball is hitting the outside of your foot as it is rolling in order for it to stop. It is highly recommended that you stop the ball when performing a chop shot fake so that it is right next to your foot once you go to plant and push away in a different direction. The chop shot fake is a very explosive skill that buys you time in two ways. First, if your shot fake is performed well, the defender will try to block the shot or turn to avoid being hit with the shot. Second, you can explode away very quickly out of the chop shot fake. Cutting the ball with the outside of your foot places the ball exactly where you would want it when you go to dribble, which makes it a lot easier for you to accelerate away with speed.

Now, something to consider is that there is an advantage to performing a shot fake poorly if you are planning to do so. Specifically, doing a shot fake that you want the defender to realize is, in fact, a shot fake will often result in the defender lunging in or relaxing. Either one will allow you to take advantage of the situation. If the defender lunges in, this provides a great opportunity to push the ball away from their foot and accelerate past them, given their momentum is going in the opposite direction yours is going. If the defender relaxes for even half a second, this gives you an opportunity to take an actual shot, pass the ball to a teammate, or continue to dribble the defender.

In summary, we have discussed the three most efficient shot fakes that you can use. First, the step on step out is to be used when you are going up the field and want to continue to go up the field, but need to create space to dribble by a defender. Second, a cut shot fake allows you to keep the ball in front of you and will enable you to push the ball and accelerate away. This can be used to continue attacking forward or to go backward. Third, the chop shot fake is where you cut the ball with the outside of your foot and use this to explode in the opposite direction from which you came. Remember that all of these shot fakes are used in order to create space for your next move, pass, or shot.

Chapter 7

Tier 2 – Cuts & Shot Fakes

Similar to the foot skills discussed in earlier chapters that have 2 Tiers, so do the type of cuts used in the different shot fakes. Similarly to foot skills, there are certain shot fakes that are more efficient than others. The Tier 2 shot fakes are the Cruyff, the V pull back, and the jump turn.

Though a seemingly funny name, the Cruyff is named after the famous soccer player Johan Cruyff who played for the Netherlands National Team, as well as for clubs Ajax and Barcelona. Johan Cruyff made this cut famous. Therefore, the move was named after him. Recall from the previous chapter where it mentioned that the cut shot fake is where the ball is cut in front of your body.

The Cruyff is when you cut the ball, but leave yourself between the defender and the ball. In essence, you are cutting the ball behind your plant leg. After the Cruyff is performed, similar to all the other shot fakes, explode away by accelerating in the direction from which you came. The Cruyff is considered a Tier 2 move because you momentarily lose sight of the ball, which can make it difficult to know precisely where the ball is when you go to turn and accelerate away from pressure. As mentioned previously, the Cruyff is best used when the defender is very close to you, within 1-2 yards, and you want to have your body between you and the ball to better protect the ball from the defender. Like the chop shot fake, this skill is used to change your direction completely. Therefore, this is not a skill to use if you desire to continue an attack forward.

The next shot fake is the V pull back. Though this may sound a bit complicated, **this shot fake is when you fake your shot and then proceed to pull the ball backward using the bottom of the foot that pretended to shoot the ball. Then, use your other leg to push the ball and accelerate forward in the other direction, hence the "V" in the V pull back.** For example, if you did the shot fake with your left foot, as you were attacking to the left, you would pull the ball back with the bottom of your left foot and then push it with your right foot to attack towards the right. Like the step on step out shot fake or the cut shot fake, you can use this move to continue attacking forward. Since you are moving the ball as part of the shot fake, this is a useful skill when the defender is very close to you and has their legs reaching in for the ball.

The last shot fake to discuss is the jump turn shot fake. For the jump turn shot fake, instead of pulling the ball back with the bottom of your foot, as you would do in the V pull back, stop the ball with the bottom of your foot as you jump past the ball, landing with both feet at the same time on the other side of the ball. **Landing with both feet at the same time on the other side of the ball allows you to explode away in the direction from which you came.** Similar to the chop shot fake, this skill is beneficial to accelerate away from the defender.

In conclusion, focus primarily on the Tier 1 shot fakes. **Only work to develop the Tier 2 shot fakes once you have perfected the Tier 1 shot fakes.** The Tier 2 shot fakes (the Cruyff, the V pull back, and the jump turn) have their places when best to be used in a game, but more often than not, the Tier 1 shot fakes will be more efficient to use in most game situations. For any of these shot fakes, they can be used just as efficiently and effectively as pass fakes or cross fakes depending on the situation you find yourself in during a game. Therefore, do not only use these fakes when pretending to shoot but when pretending to pass and cross the ball too.

As it has been stated before, perfect practice makes perfect, so work on your form with these shot fakes and cuts.

Remember that your shot fake must look exactly like your shot to ensure that the defender will either flinch and turn a little bit (buying you time) or that the defender will lunge out and try to stop your shot (allowing you to accelerate in a different direction to score, pass, or cross the ball). If the different Tiers and each of the skills within the Tiers seem like a lot to absorb at once, consider heading to UnderstandSoccer.com/free-printout in order to receive an outstanding summary that organizes and explains each of these skills in the different Tiers.

Chapter 8

Beating a Defender

To travel past a defender when dribbling, make sure that you aggressively push the ball and explode away after doing a foot skill. This chapter is an excerpt from the previous book in the Understand Soccer Series – *Soccer Shooting & Finishing: A Step-by-Step Guide on How to Score*. **The four essential reasons for an aggressive push are:**

1. **It provides space between you and the defender.** Therefore, you will have slightly more time to pick your head up to see where the goalie is and where to aim your shot.

2. If you accelerate after pushing the ball, you will have more speed running to the ball. **If you have more speed running to the ball, you are naturally going to have a more powerful shot.** For example, imagine you are standing still and you strike a shot with your foot planted next to the ball versus having a good three to four step run up on the ball. You will kick it a lot further with a running start when your momentum, your body, and your hips can travel through the ball when you strike your shot.

3. An aggressive push past the defender gets you closer to the net. **The closer you are to the net, the more accurate you will be as the net becomes bigger.** Additionally, being closer to the net, the goalie is going to have less time to react to stop your shot.

4. **When you explosively push the ball closer to the net, the goalkeeper will have less time to react to your shot.** If the goalie has less time to react to your shot, the greater the chance that your shot will go in. Now, keep in mind that pushing the ball too far will give the ball to the opponent's goalkeeper.

   Pushing the ball past a defender is best suited for when you have just performed a foot skill. You push the ball with the outside portion of your laces about 5-7 yards behind the defender. Please keep in mind faster players can afford to push the ball further than slower players. Also, a 5-7 yard push works great when you are going against only one defender, but if there is another defender behind the defender you are approaching, you would want to first use a foot skill. Then, you would use a smaller push of the ball that will only go 2-3 yards. This will help you avoid pushing the ball into the supporting defender's feet.

It is critical that you go into a game with the mindset that you will beat defenders that will allow you to take shots. If your current mindset has you a little bit scared to go against a defender 1v1, you are likely not going to be successful. You have to have confidence in yourself, so as you read this book and implement the tips, tricks, tweaks, and techniques this book mentions, you will gain confidence in your ability to beat a defender and strike a quality shot on net.

Consider the fact that a defender is typically running backward when you are going against them. **Therefore, it is crucial to understand that a defender running backward will not be as quick as an attacker running forward.** As a result, an attacker's speed is critical because the higher the pace the forward attacks with, the harder it will be for the defender to keep up while staying balanced. Additionally, when you explode past a defender, there is a brief moment when the defender is transitioning from running backward to turning their body to run forward to keep up with you. If your initial push is explosive enough, the defender will not have time to transition their body's momentum from running backward to running forward quickly enough to stop you. Watch Eden Hazard, the Chelsea and Belgium National team member to see a player that can effectively take first touches and push the ball efficiently past defenders, seemingly with ease.

Furthermore, you do not have to be entirely past the defender to take a shot. All you need is just a little bit of space to create a shot that is effective and on target. If the defender has been covering you well during the game, shooting into their shins/ankles is not going to help your team at all, but keep in mind that you miss 100% of the shots you do not take. It is much more important for a soccer team to try to increase the volume of its shots because more shots result in more chances for the ball to go in.

Let us play out a situation; a team that takes 30 shots in a game compared to a team that takes five really good shots. The team that takes 30 shots is still probably going to win because there are more opportunities for the goalie to accidentally make a mistake, for the shooting team to have a lucky shot, or for the goalie to give up a rebound resulting in a teammate shooting the ball into the back of the net.

Chapter 9

Dribbling with Both Feet

As a soccer player, your primary objective is to beat the other team in the game. Therefore, if the goal is to win, you should be willing to do what it takes to place yourself in better situations in order to succeed.

As a result, it is important that you are able to use both of your feet. Just because you have two feet, I am not suggesting that you have to be able to dribble with both of them equally. **However, both feet should be able to do the skill needed to dribble by the defender, to pass the ball, to cross the ball, or to take a shot on net.** Using both feet allows you to become more elusive and unpredictable.

Anytime you are performing a drill, weaving in and out of cones at practice, or going up against the defender, you can successfully dribble through or past the obstacle with both feet. **Having a few mastered moves in situations where you are forced to use your opposite foot will be enough for the defender to have to respect it.** It is recommended that you perform the drill in one direction and then switch up the direction of the cones so if you were using right-footed jab steps, now you will be using a left-footed jab step. If you were using right-footed cut shot fakes, now you can use left-footed cut shot fakes and right to left self-passes become left to right self-passes. Being able to dribble with both feet gives you more options for where you can go with the ball and how you can dribble around a defender. As mentioned in the book *Soccer Shooting and Finishing: A Step-by-Step Guide on How to Score*, it is very important that you can shoot with both feet and related to this book, it is just as important that you can dribble with both feet.

Whatever space the defender is giving you, you need to be able to use it efficiently. If the defender is defending you well, you will still be able to create space with your foot skills and abilities. **Countless players that I have played with and have trained are only good with one foot, usually their right foot and this makes them incredibly predictable and easy to stop.** All a defender needs to do is reduce their ability to attack to their right. If they cannot go to their right side, they cannot use their right foot to shoot and you have made them an ineffective soccer player. On the other hand, a good defender will notice if you are only good with one foot and make sure that you cannot use your dominant foot as effectively as you would hope to in a game.

Let us play out an example. **If you only dribble with your right foot, right-footed skills will often move the ball to your left foot, making it easier to shoot with your left foot.** As a result, if you cannot dribble with your left foot, you will often find it difficult to move the ball to the right side of your body, so that you can use your right foot to shoot. The opposite applies for left-footed soccer players.

Furthermore, just as much as being able to practice with it and develop it is essential, but having a quality mindset about your opposite foot is just as important too. **Also, notice that in this entire chapter, it was never called it a "weak foot," only your "opposite foot."** Often, a person will believe their opposite foot is weak and there is little they can do to improve it simply because they call their opposite foot their "weak foot." This limiting belief makes it so a player does not take steps to improve their abilities to use their opposite foot. It is highly recommended that you always call it your opposite foot so that you do not associate that negative meaning with "weak" in your mind and ultimately into your game.

Look at the great soccer players of all time, it is difficult to find a handful of the greatest that could only use one foot because the greatest soccer players know that being able to go in either direction or use either foot will allow them to increase the probability of success on the field and furthering their playing career. Since you are a player, parent, or coach reading this book, you would not be spending the time learning this information if you did not care about improving. Therefore, one of the quickest things that you can do to grow and to advance your game on the field is to focus on developing your opposite foot so you can use either foot when you are dribbling the ball up the field and past the opposing team.

Chapter 10

Do Not Be Selfish

In soccer, it is essential that your teammates do not consider you as a selfish soccer player. Given that you are learning from the steps in this book to improve your ability to dribble the ball, you will be more likely to want to dribble past players instead of immediately looking for an open pass. **As a result, if you start to consistently dribble instead of pass as you are developing your foot skills, many of your teammates might begin to view you as being selfish.** To clarify, if being selfish in specific instances will allow you to score, which will further your team's objective, then you can make the argument that this selfishness is needed and helpful to win.

However, when you have a blatantly obvious opportunity to pass the ball to your teammate that will make it easier for them to score than you, and you decide that it is better for you to keep dribbling, these are the situations that you should avoid. These situations result in teammates thinking that you are in it for yourself, which diminishes the trust they have with you. **Always keep in the back of your mind that your team's principal objective is to win the game.** Therefore, if a pass will better serve your team, pass the ball. If dribbling the ball will better help your team, then dribble the ball. The situation determines if you will be called selfish by your teammates. If you are a forward attacking towards the opposition's net and there are no teammates lateral with you or in front of you to pass the ball, then in these situations, it is entirely appropriate for you to take on a defender by using your foot skills to create space to fire off a shot. Another case that it is acceptable to dribble is when a poor pass has been played to you and the defender is practically on top of you. Use your foot skills to escape this uncertain situation as it is more difficult to pick your head up to find someone to pass to when the other team's player is smothering you.

You may be wondering if there is ever a situation where it is acceptable to be blatantly selfish. **As a general rule of thumb in soccer, you do not want to be selfish. However, if you observe the most celebrated soccer players that have ever graced the pitch, you will notice that there is a bit of selfishness to their character and in their play.** They knew to develop as a soccer player, they needed the ball at their feet. In order to score, they need the ball at their feet. To be recognized by scouts, coaches, parents, and other players, they understood that they need the ball at their feet. You may consider this as a player that is merely taking responsibility for their team, but understand that many others will see it as you are placing your own interests before the team's interests.

Therefore, depending on where you are in your career and depending if there are scouts or potential coaches at a game, it can understandably sway you to be a bit more selfish to show off your abilities. Luckily, there is an easy workaround for this. **Make sure you are always demanding and yelling for the ball because if you possess the ball more often, you will have more opportunities to show your skills off.**

Also, you will have more opportunities to pass the ball, so that the coaches and scouts can see your abilities with the ball and passing abilities. **Furthermore, when you are not in an actual competitive game, such as when you are playing in practice, playing pickup soccer, or with a bunch of your friends while working on your soccer skills, it is more appropriate to be a bit more selfish.** Again, the underlying belief is that to become better at soccer, you need the ball at your feet. Recall the pyramid at the beginning of this book and consider diving into one of the soccer specific sections. Pick a few of the skills in that area to work on and emphasize them when you are practicing.

Obviously, this is not true for all things. While reading this book, a soccer ball is probably not at your feet and you are still becoming better at soccer by increasing your knowledge of how to play the game. In general, however, the reason certain countries can produce top soccer talent is that they ensure their youth players have many opportunities for significantly more touches on the ball. 3v3 and 5v5 games result in foreign players being more confident in game situations.

It does take a bit of experience to find the happy medium between passing the ball, dribbling to beat a defender, and shooting to score. **Do not be the player that expects to win the game for your team each time you touch the ball.** It will be detrimental for your team if every time you obtain the ball, you have to dribble it before you make a pass. Remember, there are plenty of opportunities to win the game for your team, but make sure you are taking the necessary steps and making the appropriate passes to place your team in high-quality situations. Use your growing dribbling and foot skills when necessary to accomplish your team's goal of winning.

In conclusion, possess the ball more to have more opportunities to dribble and pass. When you are caught in tight situations or you are the person with the ball attacking the defender with no options to pass laterally or up the field, then dribble in this situation. It is important to consider the teammates that you are playing with. **If you are the least talented one on the field then it is more appropriate for you to pass more. If you are the most talented player on the field, it is appropriate for you to dribble a bit more** when necessary to give your team a quality chance at scoring. Furthermore, use practice time, pick-up games, and scrimmages to be a bit more selfish, knowing that more touches on the ball and learning from mistakes that you have made will increase your abilities when game time comes around.

Chapter 11

1v1s

A soccer player that can go up against one defender and win at least 80% of the time is very rare in soccer. These players are coveted by coaches because they know that this player will be able to create space away from the opposition to take more shots on net. **More shots generally means a much higher probability for goals or rebounds that turn into goals.** Please understand that you still want to make good decisions and avoid dribbling just to take unreasonable shots. Therefore, as a soccer player developing your skills to perform in 1v1 situations successfully, **consider the following three things:**

1. Use a foot skill.
2. Attack with speed.
3. Aim to use your dominant foot to shoot.

First, use a foot skill!!! Using a foot skill to create space is one piece of advice that should most definitely be followed in a 1v1 situation, but sadly few players actually do. Most wait to pass the ball to a supporting teammate or try to outrun the opposition by kicking the ball past the defender and using his or her speed. Specifically, use a jab step or a scissor to fake as if you are going to your opposite foot. Done correctly, this will enable you to have created a foot or two of space to explode forward with your dominant foot. An attacking skill where the defender is backpedaling often lures the defender to commit to going in the wrong direction. If the defender goes the wrong way, he or she will be off balance, which significantly increases the chance for you to take your shot without it being blocked or even for you to dribble entirely past the defender, allowing you a one-on-one opportunity with the opponent's goalie.

Next, attack with speed. A 1v1 situation is excellent for a forward that usually has two or three defenders covering them. Attack as if you do not have any support coming, but do not be afraid to make a pass if you see a teammate out of the corner of your eye. Do not look straight down at the ball when dribbling. Instead, look five or so yards past the ball to see a teammate or potentially another defender. In addition, occasionally take a quick glance to see where the goalkeeper is because, in 1v1 situations, goalies will often come further out of their net, which may present you an excellent opportunity to chip the ball over them.

Goalies will often creep up the field and out of their net. They realize that a forward is trained to dribble past a defender and has a pretty good chance of winning the 1v1 battle against the defender. This frees the attacker to have a shot or dribble towards the net, so the goalie will want to come out a little bit to cut down the angle of the shot. If the goalkeeper is standing square in the middle of the net when the striker shoots, there is very little chance that they will save shots that are close to either of the posts. However, if the goalie comes out and cuts the angle off, they are limiting the amount of net into which the striker can shoot. **The speed after the skill is critical to create the space and separation between you and the defender.**

Jog by the defender and they will sprint to catch up. Sprint by the defender and you will most likely not have to beat them again on that specific attempt to score.

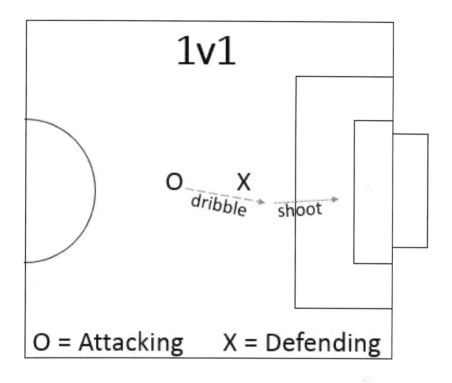

Lastly, whenever you have a 1v1 situation while attacking towards the other team's net, your goal should be to take your shot with your dominant foot. Obviously, the foot that you are more comfortable using will provide a more accurate and powerful shot on target compared to your opposite foot. **In a 1v1, because only one person is defending you, a good striker will go in the direction that he or she wants, as shown in the image, when the defender is directly in front of them.** Therefore, if you are right-footed, practice those left-footed jab steps and scissor to ensure that the ball ends up on your right foot when you go to shoot.

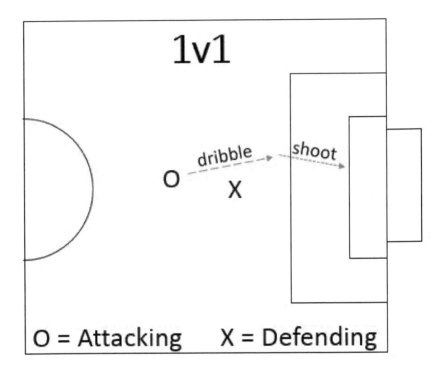

However, you do not want to go to your dominant foot 100% of the time because, on occasion, the defender will be letting you go to your opposite foot by completely cutting off your path up the field towards your dominant foot, as shown in this image. **In a situation where the defender gives you a lot of space to your opposite foot, take it because you will be able to push well past the defender to ensure that you can take a shot with your opposite foot.** Since you will have much more space than going to your dominant foot, it will be easier for you to take a powerful and well-driven shot on target when you go to strike the ball. Otherwise, use a jab step, scissor, or inside of the foot shot fake to help create space to enable you to travel to your dominant foot. Also, consider if you have gone against that defender already in the game. Use the information on what makes your opponent uncomfortable, what worked, and what you think may work to increase your chance of beating them.

To conclude, your objectives when attacking in a 1v1 are to use a skill to create space, attack with speed to take the space that the foot skill created, and more often than not, use a foot skill that will move the ball to your dominant foot when you go to strike the ball. Capitalize on 1v1s to ensure you score a goal for your team and build your confidence as a soccer player. This chapter may also be found in the previous book in the Understand Soccer Series – *Soccer Shooting & Finishing: A Step-by-Step Guide on How to Score.* 1v1s are related to dribbling and foot skills as much as they are related to shooting and finishing. If you found this chapter helpful, pick up the *Soccer Shooting & Finishing* Book for chapters on 2v1s, 1v2s, and 2v2s, among other topics.

Chapter 12

Turning with a Defender on Your Backside

As a soccer player that is looking to score, you will often find yourself with your back turned towards the very thing you are aiming to score in, the other team's net. **It is incredibly important that you are able to effectively receive a pass, turn your body, and explode up the field.** Ideally, you should be able to do this all in one motion. Recently, this topic was the main focus of a training session for one of my trainees, Kylie Kade, who has aspirations of playing for the United States Women's National Team. **Therefore, steps to consider when turning with a defender on your backside are:**

1. Look over your shoulder before you receive the pass to feel comfortable demanding the ball if you have space and believe you can do something productive for your team. **(Have your head on a swivel.)**
2. **Use your arm** to help you balance and prevent the opposing team's defender from going around you to cut off the pass.
3. Either have your shoulders pointed directly at the ball when it is coming towards you (so that you are not showing which way you are going) or **be tricky by using your body to fake like you are going one way when you are planning to push the ball in the other direction**.

4. Use the outside of your foot to push the ball. **It is not a first touch you are looking to take but a first step that includes the first touch,** so that you can accelerate away more quickly from the defender.

First, it cannot be stressed enough that you should look behind your shoulder when you are preparing to receive a pass. Depending on the situation, it may be best to just hold the ball and wait for support. A quick look will allow you to know where you should push the ball or even if you should request a pass at all from a teammate. Do not twist at the hips to look behind you because this takes too much time. **Only turn your head by using your neck to make sure that you can take a swift look at the field and the players behind you.** If you do this and determine that you have space to attack then yell for the ball and demand that it be passed to you.

Second, you will very rarely be called for having your hands on an opponent. As such, when you are ready to receive the pass with your back facing the net you are looking to score in, keep your arm up for balance, but especially to hold back the defender to ensure you are the one to receive the pass and not the other team. Having your arm up does not mean that you should hold onto them, but should place your forearm against them to slow their attempt to travel around you to intercept the ball. Also, having your arm up allows you to feel if the defender is more towards either side of you, which would factor into your decision on how to turn.

Third, never show the defender where you are going by revealing it to him or her with your body. When turning with your back to the goal and a defender is on your backside, either have your shoulders pointed directly at the ball when it is coming towards you or be deceptive and use your body to fake as if you are going one way when you are planning to push the ball in the other direction. Having your body pointed directly at the ball does not reveal to the defender which way you are going, which is good, but the defender will only commit to going in a direction that they believe you will be pushing the ball. This is why it is so effective to use your body to pretend as if you are going one way, while your real intentions are to go the other way.

Therefore, have your shoulders turned slightly in the direction that you want your defender to think you are going. **Many defenders read the opposing player's body language as much as they read where the ball is currently located when judging how to stop a player attacking with the ball.** Therefore, if you show the defender the direction that you are not going, they will often overcommit to the wrong side. If the defender commits to the wrong side, it will make it very easy for you to beat the defender without worrying about slowing the speed of play or having the defender steal the ball.

When taking a deceptive first touch, there are two options. First, if you are looking to take your first touch in the space to the area behind you to the right, then turn your body/shoulders slightly to left (so the defender will assume you are going to the left) and raise your right leg so it looks like you will be pushing to the left. However, at the last second, before receiving the pass, move your right leg across your body so that you can push with the outside of your foot to go to the space behind you to the right. Do the opposite of this if you looking to go to the space behind you on the field, to the left. The second option for when you want to deceive a defender into thinking you are going to the area to the left behind you, when you are really looking to go to the right is start by pointing your body/shoulders slightly to the left, then look like you are going to push the ball with your left foot.

However, pretend to push the ball with your left a bit too early, so that you can plant that left leg on the ground, and raise your right leg across your body to push the ball with the outside of your right foot. Think of this as a jab/feint where you miss receiving the ball with your left foot and take it with your right. You can choose which move suits you better. The first option takes some flexible ankles and the ability to pivot with the plant foot that is already on the ground. The second option provides for a very stable plant of the left foot just after you have purposely missed the ball to allow for quick acceleration out with your right foot. Therefore, the second option is the preferred option, but please try both and see which one is more fluid for you.

Fourth, it is ideal to use the outside of your foot to push the ball when turning into the space diagonally behind you because it allows you to take your first touch/step without having your legs crossed when you plant to explode away. Crossing your legs is very unathletic and should be avoided when possible as it is hard to explode with speed and it is easier to become unbalanced. It is especially important to be active and on the toes/balls of your feet to be ready for any pass.

To take a smaller touch when turning with a defender on your backside, take your first touch/step with the outside of your foot toward your toes because this is a softer area on your foot and the ball will not bounce off as powerfully. For a bigger touch, use the portion of your outside foot towards your heels to push the ball since the ball will be pushed with the harder area of the outside of your foot. **Push the ball far enough to create space between you and the defender.**

Combine these four steps to become a deceptive forward that is quickly able to make progress up the field, even if their back is turned to it. Turning with your back towards the net you need to score on is a skill that most soccer players never learn. However, if this skill is mastered, it will place you in an elite class of forwards that are confident and able to control the ball. Several players to watch for good examples and that are known for their ability to be a point man (a big presence capable of winning balls out of the air and connecting passes for smaller/quicker players) are Karim Benzema, Edinson Cavani, Gonzalo Higuaín, Olivier Giroud, and Zlatan Ibrahimović.

Chapter 13

The Nutmeg

I want to start out this chapter by saying though it feels like you dominated another player when you complete a nutmeg on an opponent, it is much more likely to be an unsuccessful attempt at pushing the ball between their legs. As mentioned in previous chapters and in previous books, we want to do the things that will give us the highest probability of success. This is why more efficient moves are found in Tier 1 and less efficient moves are located in Tier 2. **Therefore, nutmegs often result in turnovers, so they are not the best thing to pursue even though many players make them out to be very important.**

Your ultimate goal is to shoot that ball into the back of the net more times than the other team does and by aiming to do a nutmeg, it will decrease your chances of being successful. As a result, avoid spending too much practice time working on going through other players, but instead focus on the ways to shoot, dribble, and pass around other players. **Think about it; you have to push the ball through the defender's legs and travel entirely to the other side of them to maintain possession of the ball.** This is the opposite of what was discussed in the 1v1s chapter of creating just enough space to take a shot. Because you have to go through the defender, your likelihood of pulling it off is significantly reduced. Let us not forget that a defender going for a nutmeg can lead to an easy goal by the other team.

Oftentimes, when you go for a nutmeg, you push the ball into the oncoming players' shins and their momentum is carrying them past you with the ball that you just gave them. They do not even need to dribble by you now because you were trying to travel to the other side of them after you hoped to push the ball between their legs. Furthermore, even if you dribble the ball through their legs, there is a high chance they will stick their arms out and block you from traveling to the other side of them. **If you do not maintain possession after pushing the ball through their legs, the nutmeg does not count!**

If you are still interested in a skill that works for me to do a nutmeg, which was taught to me by my mentor Aaron Byrd, then use a slightly modified V pull back. If the ball is outside your left shoulder, instead of using your left foot to pull the ball back, use your right foot to start pulling it back. Beginning the V pull back with the opposite foot that is closest to the defender will prompt the defender to try to place their foot in the lane that you would pull the ball in if you were going to do the V pull back. At the last second, pull the ball back only slightly then proceed to push it between the defender's open legs. This skill has allowed me to nutmeg (meg) many opposing players and many trainees. Going for nutmegs is something that I might do once in an entire season.

I have a friend that is the king of the "meg," Youssef Hodroj. On the one hand, his recommendation is similar to mine in that he also recommends rarely going for a nutmeg in a game because it is too risky. On the other hand, he believes that a nutmeg is an important concept to the art of humiliating your opponent and getting into their head. **In reality, if you are able to complete a nutmeg on an opposing player, then there is a high chance that he or she will keep their legs closer together, which will make it easier for you to push by them later in the game.**

Furthermore, Youssef is quick to point out that soccer is a very situational game and depends heavily on your positioning relative to the defender. It is best to understand that skills that you use force them to plant heavily on one foot, which will cause them to reach for the ball with their other foot. This reach provides a large space between their feet increasing the chance you can push the ball through their legs and maintain possession of it on the other side of them.

In short, use the nutmeg very rarely. When you are with friends or playing in a pick-up game, this is an optimal time to work on the skill that will allow you to do a nutmeg on your opponent. The Nutmeg does not fall into Tier 1 or Tier 2 of the skills mentioned in this book because it is a move that often does not work. In fact, you often end up pushing the ball into the defender's shins as his or her momentum is carrying them towards your net with little chance of you being able to slow them down because your momentum is taking you in the opposite direction.

Chapter 14

Why Most Skills Are Unnecessary

As you have been reading, you may have noticed that there are several skills that you have probably heard of are not included in the contents of this book. This is for a good reason because **many skills are distracting at best for a soccer player.** In life, you can easily have too many things going on. The more things you have on your plate, the less you can focus on each one of the items individually. Focusing on too many things in soccer is no different. If you start spending considerable practice time on skills that are not very useful in a game, this will take away practice time from the important skills that you will need in every single game. Ultimately, spreading yourself too thin will result in you being a "jack of all trades (skills) but a master of none." In soccer, if you can master the Tier 1 foot skills, the Tier 1 shot fakes and potentially the step over, you will have all the necessary tools to dribble your way through the other team.

Though the Rainbow, Akocha, Elastico/Snake, Roll to Heel, Hocus Pocus, Ronaldo Chop, Rivelino... are exciting foot skills to learn and to help develop your touch, they are not needed. And yes, for those of you who have never heard of these before, these are all names of skills that you can perform, among many others. If you are curious about any of them, feel free to search for them on YouTube, but only to know what they are, but not to practice them. Consider practicing them only if you can perform the jab step, the self-pass, and the three types of shot fakes 10 times each, without making a single mistake. Even then, you would be better off mastering the Tier 2 skills, perfecting your ability to shoot, developing your ability to pass and receive, and learning how to dispossess the other team of the ball efficiently.

To sum up, most skills that you may see or hear about are unnecessary and only worth practicing if you have perfected the skills in the different Tiers mentioned in this book and the other topics covered in separate books as shown on the Individual Soccer Player's Pyramid. Similarly to how playing the Crossbar Challenge or working on Bicycle Kicks can be detrimental, as discussed in the book Soccer Shooting & Finishing, the Rainbow, Akocha, Elastico/Snake, Roll to Heel, Hocus Pocus, Ronaldo Chop, Rivelino,... can hinder you too. There is a concept in Economics called "opportunity cost" that is perfect to understand in this situation.

Specifically, opportunity cost is the cost of not doing certain things because you chose to do something else. The cost of the fancy skills mentioned previously is too high because you have to give up practice time on what is most important. Be protective of your practice time and emphasize the abilities that are most commonly used in a game to ensure that you become an all-star soccer player as quickly as possible.

Chapter 15

The Field/Terrain Matters

Considering that the goal of dribbling is to help your team score, **the field on which you are playing and the weather conditions you are playing in make a big difference.** Whether it is 75°F and sunny or 35°F with freezing cold rain, these factors have a massive impact on whether you should dribble a lot or only a little in a game.

Most games, practices, and scrimmages will be played in relatively nice weather. The soccer season's timeline is often spaced out to where you are avoiding those cold weather months. **Therefore, most of your touches on the ball tend to be when the weather conditions are good or you are inside of a building, where the weather conditions are consistent and do not have an impact on the game whatsoever.** Due to the fact that most of your practice time is done in relatively comfortable temperatures and probably on well-groomed fields, if you find yourself playing in a game where the field is rough, the grass is too long, or the weather conditions are sub-optimal, this is a situation where you want to reduce the number of foot skills used during the game. Since so many of your touches are done in a weather controlled environment or on a perfectly groomed field, your touch will be off in a game where the ball is wet or the field is bumpy.

Poor fields or weather conditions cause your dribbling abilities to be lessened and increase the chance that the opposing team will be able to steal the ball as you attempt your foot skills in the game. Therefore, you will not want to rely heavily on your foot skills and dribbling skills in a poor weather condition game. **You can use these type of games to your advantage by understanding that simple passes will often be better.** When it is raining outside, take more shots on net knowing the ball may skip causing the goalie to misjudge the ball. Similarly, the goalie will be able to block shots but give up many rebounds because the ball is slippery, making it easy for your team to convert those rebounds into goals.

A good example involves professional soccer clubs across Europe. When a home team is playing an opponent that has excellent foot skills, the stadium managers will have their soccer field watered just before game time. Pre-game field watering causes for a ball that is more difficult to dribble, which will reduce the opponent's foot skill and dribbling abilities.

Similarly, if it is 95°F out and there is a blazing sun, this is also an extreme playing condition that requires smarts on your part. Specifically, you will lose energy more quickly and **few things deplete your energy reserves as much as trying to**

use your foot skills to dribble around several defenders on the other team. Think about it, with all of the accelerating required after many of the foot skills, this explosive push and acceleration will tire you. In 95°F weather, it will tire you 2-3 times as fast. Therefore, hot games are great opportunities to let the ball do the work, by creating space with your passing and receiving abilities. Check out the fourth book in the Understand Soccer Series, *Soccer Passing & Receiving: How to Work with Your Teammates*, to learn the tips and tricks to take your passing and receiving to the next level.

Now, considering that you will have times where you are playing in poor weather conditions, **it does help to practice in those conditions**. You will be more comfortable with the ball at your feet and using foot skills on a bumpy field, during a rainstorm, through high winds, or on days where the temperature is very high. Knowing that you have practiced in these conditions will give you the confidence and the experience to make you a more well-rounded player, no matter the weather conditions. Please understand that a good soccer player will recognize how the weather conditions will impact their game and adjust their playing style accordingly.

Chapter 16

How to Practice Dribbling and Fast Footwork

With all things, <u>perfect</u> practice makes perfect. When it comes to soccer, it is no different. Practicing to be a good dribbler with the proper form will surely make you a better dribbler. Therefore, the following is a fast footwork warm-up that I will often have my trainees perform when I am first working with them to see how good their technical abilities are. Also, the fast footwork acts as an excellent warm-up for 10 or so minutes in the first portion of practice. **This warm-up increases the number of touches that a player gets on the ball.** Set up a cone on the field that is about 15 to 20 yards away from another cone on the field so that the fast footwork can be practiced in between the cones as follows:

1. Small Dribbles
2. Speed Dribbles
3. Outs and Ins
4. Push Stop
5. Self-Passes
6. Roll Touch
7. Rolls
8. Roll Stop
9. Step On Step Outs
10. Touch Scissor

1. **Small Dribbles** - With your toes pointed down and in, push the ball forward with the bone of your foot. Go for as many touches as possible from one cone to the other. Then, switch feet and repeat.

2. **Speed Dribbles** - With your toes pointed down and in, push the ball forward with the bone of your foot. Go for a touch every single step from one cone to the other. Then, switch feet and repeat.

3. **Out and Ins** - With your toes pointed down and in, push the ball diagonal with the bone of your foot (out) and then cut the ball with the inside of your foot (in). Go for as many touches as possible from one cone to the other. Then, switch feet and repeat.

4. **Push Stop** - With your toes pointed down and in, push the ball forward with the bone of your foot then stop the ball with the bottom of the same foot that pushed the ball, then immediately switch feet and repeat.

5. **Self-Passes** - using both feet, perform a pass from one foot to the next. The foot that receives the pass pushes the ball forward with the inside of the foot. Then using the same foot that pushed it, your next touch passes the ball back across your body so you can push the ball forward with the other foot.

6. **Roll Touch** - Facing forward, roll the ball across your body, then take a touch up with the opposite foot. Then with the opposite foot, roll the ball back across your body and push the ball up with the foot that did not roll the ball.

7. **Rolls** - With your body turned to the right and the side of your shoulder pointed towards the opposite cone, roll the ball using the bottom of your foot. Repeat with the opposite foot. When rolling the ball with the bottom of your foot, always use the bottom of your toes. Using the bottom of your heel or the bottom of the middle of your foot will not allow you to reach as far, your foot is more likely to bounce off the ball, and you have the most nerve endings in your foot in your toes. Having the most nerve endings in your toes means your toes have the best feel for the ball.

8. **Roll Stop** - Similarly with your shoulders turned sideways, roll the ball with the bottom of your toes, but stop the ball with the inside of your opposite foot. Then, with the same foot that rolled the ball, roll the ball again. Repeat this with the left foot.

9. **Step On Step Outs** - With your toes pointed down and in, push the ball diagonal with the bone of your foot. Then, with the same foot that pushed the ball, stop it with the bottom of your toes. Then, immediately push the ball diagonal with your other foot and stop it with the bottom of the same foot that pushed the ball. Then repeat going back and forth using both feet.

10. **Touch Scissor** - Using only one foot, touch the ball forward with your toes pointed down and in. Then, with the same foot do a scissor. Then, move the ball with the same foot and do another scissor.

Note: Set up a line of cones with each cone spaced one yard apart. Perform these fast footwork skills between cones to increase your precision and accuracy of your touch.

One thing that is so exciting about this warm-up is that it does warm up a player significantly. A soccer player is moving a lot and taking many touches. In fact, in the book *The Compound Effect*, research was done on why Brazil can consistently turn out great soccer players at a higher rate than other countries. What was found was as children are growing up in Brazil, they grow up playing in games that have much smaller numbers. They are much more likely to play in a 4v4 or 5v5 in their leagues and competitions. The low number of players in each game is the opposite of what American children have become accustomed to, who at a relatively young age, are already playing in 11v11 games. You are likely already seeing the problem with this. **The more people on the field means the fewer touches any of the soccer players will have on the ball.**

To become better with the ball, you need to take more touches and the Brazilian kids on average are taking two to three touches in a game for every one touch an American child obtains. Whether these are futsal or beach soccer games, both styles are 5-a-side and emphasize good ball control, agility, and a touch of finesse. As a result, it is no surprise that they are often much more skilled and better on the ball than the American youth players. **That is why the fast footwork above is so important because it allows yourself and your players to have a ton more touches on the ball that you or your team would not have had the opportunity to have otherwise.**

More touches on the ball will increase a soccer player's confidence with the ball. This increased confidence with the ball makes it more likely for them to want to actually dribble and develop their foot skills. Whereas, players that are lacking confidence, try to kick the ball away as soon as they receive it, so they hopefully can trick the other people into thinking that they are good soccer players, when in reality, they are really struggling and lacking the self-esteem that would allow them to improve.

In conclusion, use the fast footwork previously discussed before a game, during a practice, or even in your basement or backyard to increase the number of touches that you will be taking every single week. **Every additional touch you take is an additional opportunity to become better and grow at a faster rate than the other players you play with and against.**

Understanding this concept is exciting because just by slightly modifying the way that you practice, you can ensure that your practice time is much better spent than your competition.

Chapter 17

Easy Drills With or Without Cones

This next chapter has easy drills to perform that allow you to practice your foot skills. The first section is a recommendation if you do not have cones. The second section is a course to set up if you do have cones.

Without Cones:
- Use two lines on the field that are 5 yards apart or the 6-yard box.
- Starting at one of the lines, push the ball with your toe down and in using the bone of your foot to the other line. (Only take one touch to travel to the other line.)
- Once at the other line, perform a shot fake. (Make sure it looks the same as your shot.)
- Then, accelerate back to the line where you started. (Only take one touch to travel back to the starting line.)
- Next, perform another shot fake. (Alternate between right and left footed shot fakes.)

Perform a set of 10 shot fakes (5 right footed and 5 left footed) starting with the cut shot fake. Perform 6 sets total. Switch the shot fake you use each time.

My recommendation is to do the Tier 1 shot fakes; cut, chop, and step on step out two times each. However, you may grow bored of doing the same skill more than once. If so, then perform the Tier 2 shot fakes (jump turn, Cruyff, and V pull back) too. Generally, this is advised against because it is better to be perfect at a few skills in soccer than to be okay at many skills.

With 9-10 Cones:

- Perform the drill as pictured below:

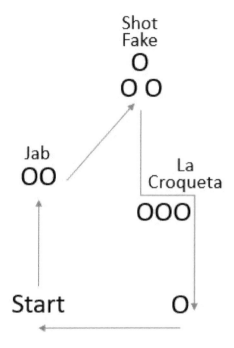

- Have each of the skills roughly 5 yards apart.
- Attack the first two cones "OO" and perform a left-footed jab step.
- Accelerate to the shot fake (The three "Os" in a triangle).
- Perform a right-footed chop shot fake.
- Accelerate with one push from your right foot to the "OOO" la croqueta.

- Do a la croqueta/self-pass by passing the ball from your right foot to your left foot.
- Accelerate to the "O" and use a right-footed chop just past the cone.
- Finally, accelerate back to the start.

Notes: Use only one push to accelerate to the next set of cones. Dribble with your head slightly up, not straight down at the ball. Make your shot fake look believable. This drill can be easily reversed to work on your skills in the opposite direction.

Conclusion

The main thing is to keep the main thing the main thing. **In soccer, the main thing to keep in mind is to develop the abilities that you are most likely to use on the field, without spending too much time on things that would be used only occasionally.** Referring back to the preface of this book, the Individual's Pyramid of Importance concept is an excellent indicator for all of the topics in soccer to emphasize how your practice time should be spent. For this book specifically, keep in mind that most of your time should be spent on the Tier 1 skills. If you master them, then maybe spend a bit of time on the Tier 2 skills. Spending time on foot skills outside of that would be much better spent on one of the topics in the different books of this series, in Tier 1, or in Tier 2 of this book.

This book and the other books in the series are meant to be read and understood, but also act as a guide to which you can refer back. Therefore, do not be afraid after you are done with this book to open it from time to time to have a refresher on the tips, tricks, tweaks, and techniques on improving your abilities. Now, keep in mind that a soccer player that wants to take their game to the next level will do whatever it takes to find the information that will help push him or her there. Then, he or she will implement the information in their practices to ensure it can be used in a game effectively.

The process of reading about how to become better, focusing on improving in practice, and then playing better in a game provides for continued growth and progress in any soccer player's career. However, be skeptical about some of the people creating YouTube videos. Many of the "soccer experts" that I have recently found on YouTube are showing poor form. This poor form results from people with little experience actually using the skills themselves in a game. This book provides a great opportunity to read the words to gain the knowledge needed to grow. Keep working to be the best player that you can be and I look forward to talking with you in the next book in the series. **If you enjoyed this book, please leave me a review on Amazon letting me know what you enjoyed.**

Bonus!

Wouldn't it be nice to have the steps in this book on an easy 1-page printout for you to take to the field? Well, here is your chance!

Go to this Link for an **Instant** 1-Page Printout:
UnderstandSoccer.com/free-printout

This FREE guide is simply a "Thank You" for purchasing this book. This 1-page printout will ensure that the knowledge you obtain from this book makes it to the field.

Free Book?

How would you like to obtain the next book in the series for free and have it before anyone else?

Join the Soccer Squad Book Team today and receive your next book (and potentially future books) for FREE.

Signing up is easy and does not cost anything.

Check out this website for more information:

understandsoccer.com/soccer-squad-book-team

Thank You for Reading!

Dear Reader,

I hope you enjoyed and learned from *Soccer Dribbling & Foot Skills: A Step-by-Step Guide on How to Dribble Past the Other Team*. I truly enjoyed writing these steps and tips to ensure you improve your game, your team's game, or your child's game.

While I was writing this book and having others critique it, I received some great insights on the book. As an author, I love feedback. Honestly, you are the reason that I wrote this book and plan to write more. Therefore, tell me what you liked, what you loved, what can be improved, and even what you hated. I'd love to hear from you. Visit UnderstandSoccer.com and scroll to the bottom of the homepage to leave me a message in the contact section or email me at Dylan@UnderstandSoccer.com.

Finally, I need to ask a favor. I'd love and truly appreciate a review of *Soccer Dribbling & Foot Skills*.

Reviews are a key part of the process to determine whether you, the reader, enjoyed my book. The reviews allow me to write more books and to continue to write articles on the UnderstandSoccer.com website. You have the power to help improve my book. Please take the 2 minutes needed to leave a review on Amazon.com at https://www.amazon.com/gp/product-review/1949511049.

Thank you so much for reading *Soccer Dribbling & Foot Skills* and for spending time with me to help improve your game.

In gratitude,

Dylan Joseph

Glossary

50-50 - When a ball is passed into pressure or cleared up the field and your teammate and a player on the opposing team each have an equal (50%) chance of taking possession of the soccer ball.

Attacking Touch - Pushing the ball into space with your first touch, which is the opposite of taking a touch where the ball stops underneath you (at your feet).

Ball Hawk - Someone usually close to the ball, in the right place at the right time, and a person who specializes in scoring rebounds.

Bat - The bone (hardest portion) of your foot.

Bent/Curved Shot - A shot that spins and curves as it goes towards the net. This shot is used when you need to shoot around defenders or goalkeepers. Though you use the bone of your foot to strike the ball instead of following through the ball with your entire body, you just follow through with your leg and cross your legs after shooting the ball.

Bicycle Kick ("Overhead Kick") - where the ball is above you and you proceed to jump up and kick the ball over your body while the ball is in the air.

Broom - In this book, it is the area on your foot towards your toes. There is space in your shoe between your toes where there is a lot more fabric and a lot less bone, which makes it a soft area on your foot, similar to the softness of a broom.

Champions League - The UEFA Champions League is an annual soccer competition involving the best of the best club teams from many of the professional leagues in Europe.

Chop - This is performed with the outside of your foot. The leg that is cutting the ball must step entirely past the ball. Then, allow the ball to hit that leg/foot, which effectively stops the ball. Having the ball stop next to your foot enables the ball to be pushed in a different direction quickly.

Counterattack ("Fast Break") - When the team defending gains possession of the ball and quickly travels up the field with the objective of taking a quick shot, so few of the other team's players can travel back to defend in time.

Crossbar Challenge - Played by one or more people where you attempt to hit the crossbar by shooting the ball from the 18-yard box.

Cruyff - Cut the ball, but leave yourself between the defender and the ball. In essence, you are cutting the ball behind your plant leg.

Cut - This is performed with the inside of your foot. The leg that is cutting the ball must step entirely past the ball. Then, allow the ball to hit that leg/foot, which effectively stops the ball. Having the ball stop next to your foot enables the ball to be pushed in a different direction quickly. Additionally, you may cut the ball so that it is immediately moving in the direction that you want to go.

Driven Shot - A shot struck with the bone of your foot, where you follow through with your entire body without crossing your legs. This is the most powerful type of shot.

Finishing - The purpose of shooting, which is to score.

Flick - Barely touching the ball to change the direction of the ball slightly for a teammate when a pass is being played to you.

Half-Volley - Striking the ball just after it hit the ground, but while the ball is still in the air.

Jab Step ("Feint," "Body Feint," "Fake," "Fake and Take," or "Shoulder Drop") - When you pretend to push the ball in one direction, but purposely miss, then plant with the foot that you missed the ball with to push the ball in the other direction.

Jockeying - When defending, backpedaling to maintain proper position in relation to the person attacking with the ball. When jockeying, the defender does not dive in for the ball. He or she waits for the ideal time to steal the ball or poke it away.

Jump Turn - Instead of pulling the ball back with the bottom of your foot, as you would do in the V pull back, stop the ball with the bottom of your foot as you jump past the ball, landing with both feet at the same time on the other side of the ball. Landing with both feet at the same time on the other side of the ball allows you to explode away in the direction from which you came.

Offside - When you pass the ball to a player on your team who is past the opposing team's last defender at the moment the kick is initiated. You cannot be offside on a throw-in or when you are on your own half of the field.

One-Time Shot - When a pass or cross is played to you and your first touch is a shot on net.

Opposite Foot - Your non-dominant foot. Out of your two feet, it is the one that you are not as comfortable using.

Outside of the Foot Shot ("Trivela") - Shooting with the bone of your foot where your toe is pointed down and in. The ball makes contact with the outside portion/bone of your foot. This shot is useful because it is quicker than a driven shot, it can provide bend like a bent shot, and is more powerful than a pass shot.

Pass Fake - Faking a pass. Keep your form the same as when you pass, including: 1) Looking at a teammate before you do a pass fake 2) Raise your passing leg high enough behind your body, so that an opponent believes you are going to kick the ball.

Pass Shot ("Finesse Shot") - A shot on the net using the inside of your foot to increase your accuracy. However, land past the ball on the follow through to increase the shot's power, similar to a shot taken with the bone of your foot.

Passing Lane - An area on the field where a teammate can pass you the ball directly, while the ball remains on the ground.

Pitch - A soccer field.

Rainbow - When you place one foot in front of the ball and the laces of the other foot behind the ball. Pin the ball between your feet and flick the ball up behind your body and over your head.

Roll ("Rollover") - Using the bottom of the toes of your foot, roll the ball parallel to the defender, crossing your feet when you plant. Then, bring your other foot around to uncross your feet and push the ball forward. The path the ball takes is the shape of an "L."

Self-Pass ("L," "Iniesta," or "La Croqueta") - Passing the ball from one foot to the other while running. Imagine you are doing a roll, but without your foot going on top of the ball. Instead, it is an inside of the foot pass from one foot and an inside of the foot push up the field with the other foot.

Set Piece ("Dead Ball") - A practiced plan used when the ball goes out of bounds or a foul is committed to put the ball back into play. The most common set pieces are throw-ins and free kicks.

Scissor - When the foot closest to the ball goes around the ball as you are attacking in a game. Emphasize turning your hips to fake the defender. To easily turn your hips, plant past the ball with your foot that is not going around the ball so that you can use the momentum of the moving ball to your advantage.

Shielding - Placing your body between the ball and the defender. With your back facing the defender and your arms wide, prevent him or her from traveling to the ball.

Shot Fake - Faking a shot. Make sure your form looks the same as when you shoot, including: 1) Looking at the goal before you do a shot fake 2) Arms out 3) Raise your shooting leg high enough behind your body, so it looks like you are going to shoot.

Square to your Teammate - Pointing your hips at a teammate.

Step On Step Out - In order to change direction, step on the ball with the bottom of your foot. Then, with the same foot that stepped on the ball, take another step to plant to the side of the ball, so that your other leg can come through and push the ball in a different direction.

Step Over - When you are next to the ball and you have your furthest leg from the ball step over the ball, so your entire body turns as if you are going in a completely different direction. The step over is best used along a sideline.

Through Ball/Run - When a pass is played into space in front of you, allowing you to continue your forward momentum.

Toe Poke/Toe Blow - Striking the ball with your big toe. The toe poke is the quickest shot, but often the most inaccurate shot.

Upper 90 - Either of the top corners on a net (corners are 90 degrees).

V Pull Back - Pull the ball backward using the bottom of your foot. Then, use your other leg to push the ball and accelerate forward in the other direction, hence the "V" in the V pull back.

Volley - Striking the ball out of the air before it hits the ground.

Wall Passing ("1-2 Passing") - A wall pass is when you pass it to a teammate and they pass it back to you with one touch similar to if you were to pass a ball against a wall.

Acknowledgments

I would like to thank you, the reader. I am grateful to provide you value and to help you on your journey of becoming a more confident soccer player, coach, or parent. I am happy to serve you and thank you for the opportunity to do so. Also, I would like to recognize people that have made a difference and have paved the way for me to share this book with you:

First, I want to thank my mother who has been a role model for what can be done when you work hard towards your goals. Her work ethic and ability to overcome adversity are truly admirable, and I look up to her for this. Also, I appreciate her feedback on wording and grammatical improvements.

Second, I would like to thank my sister who, though she is younger than me, I look up to her for her ability to be positive around negative people and situations. During her career, she was a dribbling and goal-scoring machine. She was a High School Varsity player during her freshman year at one of largest high schools in the state and was known for her upper 90 goals.

Thirdly, I would like to thank the content editors and fellow soccer players Tom Catalano, Antonio Denkovski, Youssef Hodroj, Toni Sinistaj, and Kevin Solorio. They reviewed this book for areas that could be improved and additional insights to share.

Lastly, I would like to thank my soccer trainer, Aaron Byrd, whose wisdom and smarts have turned me into the player I am today. His guidance and knowledge about this game have made it so that I can pass this knowledge on to rising stars, coaches looking to grow their understanding of soccer, and caring parents!

Many thanks,

Dylan Joseph

What's Next?

Each of the chapters in this book aims to increase your ability to dribble past the other team. Implementing the tips, tricks, tweaks, and techniques you just read in this book will surely help you in achieving your dreams to become an outstanding soccer player. If you enjoyed the contents of this book, please visit my website at UnderstandSoccer.com to let me know what you were most excited to read.

I aim to create a book on nearly every topic covered in the first book in the series *Soccer Training: A Step-by-Step Guide on 14 Topics for Intelligent Soccer Players, Coaches, and Parents* and would love for you to answer the **one question poll** at UnderstandSoccer.com/poll to help me determine what area of soccer you want to improve next. Your vote on the upcoming books in the series will help determine what book is to follow!

Made in the USA
Columbia, SC
14 January 2020